Lost in New Zealand

Lost in New Zealand

CRAIG POTTON

craig potton publishing

LOST IN NEW ZEALAND

Maud Moreland came to New Zealand from England in the early 1900s to join her brother, the Reverend CH Moreland, who was then the principal of Christ's College in Christchurch.

In 1906 she and her brother undertook a remarkable five-week trip on horseback, from Christchurch over Arthur's Pass, down through South Westland, over Haast Pass and then home to Canterbury. Her account of the trip was subsequently published in a book Through South Westland, *from which the following extracts have been taken.*

They have been selected as an introduction to Lost in New Zealand *because they so eloquently capture the sense of wonder and delight that can be had from encountering New Zealand's natural world. Though over 100 years have passed since Maud Moreland completed her journey, these wild places are still to be found in New Zealand, and are still just as extraordinary. It is my hope that* Lost in New Zealand *can serve as a reminder of, and an inspiration for your own encounters with these beautiful parts of our country.*

Craig Potton

OUT OF THE TOWN and along the dusty white road lined with trim houses, and gardens aglow with colour: on to country roads less dusty and with fewer and fewer houses, we rode forth one morning. It was six o'clock. The road-side herbage was drenched with dew. A grey-blue haze lay all over the wide Canterbury plains which seemed to stretch away to the farthest horizon, tall gum trees and fir plantations round the homesteads breaking the monotony of their flatness. Everywhere the crops were ripening to harvest; another week's sunshine and the wheatfields that waved all golden now would be cut. Fruit ripened in the orchards, and summer was at its height.

It was a blue day. All objects, near and far, were tinged with blue under the New Zealand sky, and as the sun got hotter, everything shimmered and trembled in the heat.

We breakfasted at a wayside inn, and rode on again, and when it grew unbearably hot we sought shelter at a little sun-baked place called Kirwee: just a few houses beside the inn, and a cabin of a railway station alongside the road—for railways and roads share the same wide tracks in the plains. Here we dawdled away the mid-day hours till teatime, and then as a little breeze sprang up we started to finish the forty-two miles to Mt. Torlesse.

The mountains had come into sight now. At first blue and featureless, then blacker and browner, the deeper valleys like splashes of purple. The first sight of their snowy tops made one forget the plains and the dusty road; our spirits rose, and we cantered fast along the wide, grassy margin. But we had lingered too long, and as we rode over an endlessly straight stretch, marked by clumps of black fir trees at regular intervals, the sudden-falling dusk came about us. The plain spread like a tawny sea to the foot-hills pushing out their purple headlands in cape and promontory:

> Darkly, like an armèd host
> Seen afar against the blue
> Rise the hills, and yellow-grey
> Sleeps the plain in cove and bay,
> Like a shining sea that dreams
> Round a silent coast.

Beyond lay a dead-white wall—a ghostly barrier of snow—between two purple ranges. All nearer objects became black and indistinct. Suddenly, behind the dead-white wall an orange light grew up, palpitating up and up past the zenith, till the night clouds overhead blazed out in gold and orange as it caught their edges. We watched it spread from bank to bank. Then came another change. The gold turned rosy red, then crimson, deeper and deeper, till all the clouds were blood-red, and we rode on in a darkening world, our eyes fixed on the glory above. It passed as suddenly as it came, and nought was left but a clear green streak of sky above the snow to show whence the glory had come; and then suddenly we realized it was dark, that we were tired, and the night grown chilly, and if we meant to arrive in any decent time that night, we must bestir ourselves. There were still seven miles to do, but we were sure of our welcome, no matter at what untimely hour we arrived. At last in the dusk we rode up to the hospitable door, and the master of Mt. Torlesse met us with a hearty greeting and bustled off the horses… After a day's rest we were rattled up betimes, and by four a.m. the Master of Torlesse was supplying our wants with hot coffee, and lecturing us on straps and the proper rolling up of our kit; and then rode with us the first three or four miles, to put us on our way. The Torlesse range lay grey and lifeless beyond the green paddocks and the crops round the homestead, and as we got among the stony hills the mist rolled down, alternating with bursts of sunshine. Everywhere stony rivers ran at the bottom of dreary valleys, with drearier hills rising up to stonier mountains, none over 6,000 feet, and all desolate. And when the afternoon came on, the rain came too, and we rode with heads down against a tearing south-west storm, that deluged us with sheets of water. Those were forty-four long miles …

But all things come to an end, and we saw the welcome end-gable of the Bealey Hotel on a rise above us …

WE MADE UP OUR minds to go on next day, and, fortunately for us, the weather proved fine.

We crossed the Waimakariri in safety, getting a beautiful view of snow mountains and glaciers at the head of the wide valley—a couple of miles, perhaps, across…

Once across, we rode up the Bealey. The gorge wound among steep mountains clothed in great part with the southern beech; waterfalls were frequent, and fine views of snow-capped ranges. Then we got to the divide called Arthur's Pass where are three small tarns lying on a mass of old moraine, which seems to fill the space between two parallel ranges. From one side of this the waters flow east, and from the other west. All this alpine meadow was beautiful with flowers: giant celmisias with satiny-white petals like enormous daisies, mingled with snow-white gentians, and the wonder of the Alps—the mountain lily [*Ranunculus lyallii*]. It is a pure white kingcup with golden centre, the leaves as large as saucers, and often the flowers are two or three inches across. As usual in the New Zealand mountains, most flowers were white. The plants here are specially interesting, because of the meeting of outliers from east and west. To a very large extent the western species do not grow on the east, except in certain places such as the Kaikouras, where the forest is very like a western forest. Farther south still, tree-ferns and pines occur; but, speaking broadly, the ranges on the east have beech forest, while the west has pine forest and a sub-tropical flora of its own.

The road zig-zagged in loops down a steep descent above a torrent. Bare, forbidding rocks and screens of loose stones ran up on one side, and presently we arrived at a place where they had all run down in a terrific rock-slide. The road was gone. A forlorn coach and one or two buggies had been abandoned there, but already a narrow track was scratched across the face of the *débris*. We led the horses over the sliding mass, and gained the undamaged road beyond. The road-menders told us of the violence of yesterday's storm which had wrecked the road, snapping off great forest trees, and strewing the track with wreckage. When we arrived at the Otira we found matters were in an even more congested state than at the Bealey. And still the people arrived! Not a bed or a towel was to be had, and at least sixty had slept there that night!

THAT WAS A GLORIOUS morning when we set out. The more sombre eastern colouring had given place to vivid greens; pine forest and ferns took the place of beech; above the gorge the snow peaks gleamed pure and sharp against the intense blue of the sky: it was enough to make the heart rejoice. And very joyous we were, as we rode down that sun-flecked woodland way, where the pinky track before us lay all mottled and barred with violet shadows. Bend after bend caught the morning sun as it poured a flood of golden light on tree-fern and unfamiliar foliage. Sometimes between the trees one caught sight of a snowy summit with mauve shadows on the snow, at the end of a purplish-blue vista. It was a fairyland of light and shade on dancing leaves, and on one side the river kept us company all the way: now swift and silent, eddying in blue-green streams, now tumbling over rocks in snowy foam.

Later I saw grander and more beautiful places, but the Otira taught me to love the road, wandering on and on beneath the trees, with its play of light and shade, its mystery and silence. The forest spoke then in an unknown tongue, but it was then I first heard its voice.

… WE STROLLED AWAY in the afternoon to see Lake Ianthe, being told it was but three-and-a-half miles off; but it seemed nearer five. At any rate it was well worth the walk. The road wound down to it through magnificent forest, where the tree-ferns expanded glorious fronds fifteen or twenty feet long, and everywhere grew a wealth of exquisite greenery. Strange new forms—new at least to our eyes—constantly attracted the attention. What the forest lacks in brilliancy of flowers, it gains in its wonderful variety of form. Except the ratas and a red honeysuckle, most of the flowers are white, or green and inconspicuous; but their perfumes are there, and every shade of green and gold and brown. Between the tall shafts of the trees we caught glimpses of a shining water, and we made our way to the shore and sat there entranced. The reflections were perfect: every leaf and twig, mountain summit, and sunset cloud lay there, as in a great looking-glass.

The snows of the distant Alps were flushing rosy-pink above the dark hills, clothed always

to their tops with trees. And as we sat and watched, the water at our feet became golden with the reflection of the rosy cloudlets floating in it. Colours like the inside of a pearl-shell blended, and faded, and the evening mists crept over all, and we turned back down the darkening forest aisles. And as we went, the moonlight laid black bars across the road, and touched the giant ferns with silver, and every sound was hushed…

… FROM THIS PLACE, named the Forks, we had a choice of ways—either to continue to the coast, visiting Okarito on its lagoon—one of the last nesting-places in the South Island of the white crane [or rather heron (*Herodias timoriensis*)]—or to turn inland along the Southern Alps. The road leads by Mapourika, most beautiful perhaps of New Zealand lakes, lying below the jagged peaks of the Minarets. Beyond, the great Franz Josef glacier winds down from those homeless wastes of ice and snow, where the Minarets and Mount Dela Bêche rear up like islands from the white expanse of the Tasman and adjoining glaciers. From their summits one looks, on the one hand across the eastern plains, and on the other over this green Western land of streams and forests, as Moses looked from Pisgah. Verily it is a Promised Land, but as yet the inheritance has not been wholly entered upon.

Mapourika is beautiful at all times in that wonderful setting of forest and mountain, but when the sunset flush on the peaks above is mirrored in the windless lake, and every tree and fern springs from its own double along the shore, I think it comes very near being Paradise …

THE BAD WEATHER HAD spent itself, and as we got ready early next morning, a cloudless sky above the snow-peaks betokened a glorious day. Good-byes were said, and we fared forth once more down the Main South Road. It made a brave show with wide, cleared margins for a couple of miles or so, then deserted us in a river-bed, and when we picked it up again, it had become a pack track. This very soon dwindled to a narrow footpath, winding into the heart of the hills. The sun slanted down through the great trees over head:

> Their forest raiment . . . . from crown to feet
>   that clothed them royally,
> Shielding their mysteries from the glare of day.

Here, we were in a world untouched by man—save for that narrow, winding track—where the very birds seemed scarce to heed our presence, and the big bush-pigeons sat and looked at us from the miro trees—too lazy to fly away. The very loneliness but added to the wondrous, mysterious charm of this forest world. On and on we rode in the dewy freshness: round steep mountain flanks, up deep gorges, along rock-cut ledges where the yellow sunshine lay bright and warm on the rocky way, catching at times vistas of high mountains towering above us, shrouded always in impenetrable bush—it was, above all things, a forest ride. Always there was the crowding undergrowth beneath—that riot of green-life, of forms strange to our eyes, beautiful in their infinite variety. And everywhere were ferns. Who shall tell of the exquisite beauty of that fernery? They seemed to grow in colonies, sometimes of one kind, sometimes of another; and every fallen mossy trunk was covered with delicate hymenophyllums, like green lace. They climbed along the living branches, they draped the brown stems of the tree-ferns from base to crown—there they live and die uncared for, generation after generation, perfect in their beauty …

I HAD ENTERED THE promised land. I had seen a world as it was before man came there; in after years it would never be quite the same again. For if I went back to it, I might not find the Fairy Land of my dreams. The forest world must give place before the fire and the axe, but the memory of it, as I saw it in my brief sojourn, can never pass away.

So, as the sun sank behind the purple barrier of the western mountains, out-lining their edges in gold: and their long shadows stretched across the plain … I said, Farewell.

Maud Moreland

PREVIOUS PAGE Alpine beech forest, West Sabine River, Nelson Lakes National Park
OVERLEAF Looking across the head of the Fox Glacier to New Zealand's highest peaks, Mt Tasman at left, and Aoraki/Mt Cook, Westland/Tai Poutini National Park

ABOVE Rainforest on the edge of Lake Mapourika, Westland/Tai Poutini National Park
LEFT Sunlight catches swamp and forest, Lake Matheson, Westland/Tai Poutini National Park

ABOVE Lowland beech forest, Paparoa National Park
RIGHT Blowhole at the Pancake Rocks, Punakaiki, Paparoa National Park

ABOVE Surge pool at the Pancake Rocks, Punakaiki, Paparoa National Park
LEFT Pancake Rocks, Punakaiki, Paparoa National Park

ABOVE AND RIGHT Seacliffs near Punakaiki, Paparoa National Park

OVERLEAF Lowland podocarp forest at Okarito with Mt Tasman and Aoraki/Mt Cook behind, Westland/Tai Poutini National Park

ABOVE Mosses and ferns on the trunk of a matai tree, Oparara, Kahurangi National Park
LEFT Early morning at Lake Mapourika, Westland/Tai Poutini National Park

ABOVE Pakihi vegetation near Punakaiki, West Coast
LEFT Rainforest near Ship Creek, South Westland

Kahikatea forest on the edge of Lake Wahapo, Westland/Tai Poutini National Park

Lowland forest and wetlands behind Ohinemaka Beach, South Westland

The head of the Fox Glacier, Westland/Tai Poutini National Park

The three peaks of Mt Haast in the foreground, Mt Tasman to the right, and Aoraki/Mt Cook behind

ABOVE The Cook River mouth and the Tasman Sea, South Westland
LEFT Rimu forest at Bruce Bay, South Westland
OVERLEAF Moon above the western faces of Mt Tasman and Aoraki/Mt Cook, Westland/Tai Poutini National Park

Norwest Lake above Lake Manapouri, Fiordland National Park

Key Summit on the Routeburn Track, with the Darran Mountains behind, Fiordland National Park

Lake Iceberg in the headwaters of the Clinton River, Fiordland National Park

ABOVE Winter at Key Summit on the Routeburn Track, Fiordland National Park
OVERLEAF Looking into Breaksea Sound, Fiordland National Park

ABOVE The Darran Mountains from the Routeburn Track, Fiordland National Park
RIGHT Mt Elliot rises above an alpine tarn on Mackinnon Pass, Milford Track, Fiordland National Park

Looking north from above the Wick Mountains, Fiordland National Park

Sunrise on Double Cone, The Remarkables, Queenstown

Schist outcrop on the Skippers Road near Queenstown

The Heath Mountains, Fiordland National Park

A winter morning on the shores of Lake Manapouri, Fiordland National Park

The Rugged Islands off the northwestern tip of Stewart Island, Rakiura National Park

ABOVE Alpine beech forest, Kepler Track, Fiordland National Park
LEFT The braided bed of the Dart River with the peaks of the Barrier Range behind, Mount Aspiring National Park

ABOVE Rainforest, Milford Track, Fiordland National Park
RIGHT Mackay Falls, Milford Track, Fiordland National Park

ABOVE Moon over the East Face of Mt Sefton, Aoraki/Mount Cook National Park
RIGHT Evening light over the Southern Alps west of Lake Wanaka

ABOVE Cabbage trees at Gillespies Beach, Westland/Tai Poutini National Park
LEFT Dusky Sound at sunset, Fiordland National Park

ABOVE Willow tree on the shore of Lake Wakatipu, Queenstown
LEFT Lake Wakatipu and the Eyre Mountains

Waterfalls following heavy rain, Milford Sound, Fiordland National Park

Bowen Falls, Milford Sound, Fiordland National Park

Sand dunes, Mason Bay, Stewart Island

ABOVE Granite boulder near the Fraser Peaks, southern Stewart Island
OVERLEAF Tussock and rainbow, Lindis Pass, between the Mackenzie Country and Otago

65

Mt Green and Mt Walter above the Tasman Glacier, Aoraki/Mount Cook National Park

Winter snow in the Richardson Mountains, Otago

Snowfall in the Hooker Valley, with Aoraki/Mt Cook behind, Aoraki/Mount Cook National Park

ABOVE The névé of the Fox Glacier below the western flanks of Mt Tasman, Westland/Tai Poutini National Park
OVERLEAF Sunrise on the eastern faces of Aoraki/Mt Cook and Mt Tasman, Aoraki/Mount Cook National Park

Early winter's morning, Lake Pukaki, Mackenzie Country

Mt Hooker and the Hooker Glacier, Hooker/Landsborough Wilderness Area, South Westland

ABOVE Sunset on the West Face of Mt Aspiring, Mount Aspiring National Park
LEFT Cloud to the west of Mt Sefton and the Main Divide, Aoraki/Mount Cook National Park
OVERLEAF The classic high country landscape of the Ahuriri River, Mackenzie Country

Evening light on the spit, Tahunanui Beach, Nelson

Archway Islands off Wharariki Beach, Golden Bay

Evening, Pakawau, Golden Bay

ABOVE Moonrise, Pakawau, Golden Bay
OVERLEAF Sunrise on Awaroa Beach, Abel Tasman National Park

ABOVE Cliffs at Oaro, Kaikoura coast
RIGHT Sunrise at Kaikoura

ABOVE Looking across the summit of Mt Manakau in the Seaward Kaikoura Range, with the North Island in the far distance
LEFT Above the Marlborough Sounds, looking across Pelorus Sound

ABOVE Ridgeline in the Spenser Mountains, Nelson Lakes National Park
LEFT Winter snow on the northwest face of Mt Una in the Spenser Mountains, Nelson Lakes National Park

The Devils Punchbowl Falls, Arthur's Pass National Park

ABOVE Blue Lake at the head of the West Sabine River, Nelson Lakes National Park
OVERLEAF Blue Lake, with Mt Ngauruhoe behind and Mt Tongariro to the right, Tongariro National Park

ABOVE Mineral deposits in the Champagne Pool, Waiotapu, Central North Island
LEFT The Pohutu Geyser at Whakarewarewa, Rotorua

Winter snow around the Crater Lake, Mt Ruapehu, Tongariro National Park

Sunset during the 1996 eruption of Mt Ruapehu, Tongariro National Park

The Waikato River just above the Huka Falls, Taupo

Volcanic ash deposits, White Island, Bay of Plenty

ABOVE The distinctive bark of kaikawaka, Tongariro National Park
RIGHT Red Crater on the Tongariro Alpine Crossing, Tongariro National Park

The Rangipo Desert near the Whangaehu Valley, with Mt Ngauruhoe on the horizon, Tongariro National Park

Emerald Lake, Tongariro Alpine Crossing, Tongariro National Park

ABOVE Tree fern in Whirinaki forest, Central North Island
LEFT A small waterfall, Whirinaki forest, Central North Island

ABOVE Mt Taranaki from the coast north of New Plymouth
LEFT The Bridal Veil Falls near Raglan, west of Hamilton
OVERLEAF The northern flanks of Mt Taranaki from the Pouakai Range, Egmont National Park

ABOVE Nikau palms, Great Barrier Island, Hauraki Gulf
LEFT Rangitoto Island at sunrise, seen from Auckland's North Shore

Cape Reinga, Northland

Kauri forest, Trounson Forest Park, Northland

ABOVE Nikau palms, Kermadec Islands
LEFT Boulders and pohutukawa trees, Little Barrier Island, Hauraki Gulf

The sweeping arc of Ninety Mile Beach, Northland

Te Paki sand dunes, northern end of Ninety Mile Beach, Northland

ABOUT NEW ZEALAND

NEW ZEALAND'S CITIES

Auckland

Described as 'a thousand suburbs in search of a city', Auckland is a metropolis sprawling over a narrow isthmus between two harbours – Waitemata and Manukau. With an area of 5300 square kilometres, yet only one million inhabitants, it has a less crowded feel than many other major cities of the world. Its waterside location has fostered the locals' love affair with sailing, earning it the nickname 'City of Sails'.

Hamilton

This is one of New Zealand's fastest growing cities and is the fourth largest urban area in the country. Placed beside New Zealand's longest river, the Waikato, it is a melting pot of more than 80 ethnic groups and has a high percentage of young people.

Napier–Hastings

These two cities are very close to each other and are sometimes referred to as the 'twin cities'. Napier's main tourist attraction is its architecture – following a big earthquake in 1931, it was rebuilt using the Art Deco style, and its buildings are today protected for their architectural uniqueness.

The country

New Zealand came into being, according to one Māori myth, when the demigod Maui hauled a giant fish from the Pacific Ocean using a hook carved from his grandmother's jawbone and his own blood for bait. It was so heavy he had to recite a magical chant to pull it to the surface. While Maui knew that he would have to make offerings to the gods in return for the fish, his impatient and jealous brothers couldn't wait and began to cut and scale the huge fish so that it writhed and thrashed in agony, its flesh becoming jagged and mutilated. At that moment the sun rose; as the rays of light hit the fish it became solid, creating a humped and rugged land. This was the North Island, or Te Ika a Maui (the fish of Maui), while the South Island was Te Waka a Maui (Maui's canoe) and Stewart Island Te Puka o te Waka o Maui (the anchor stone of Maui's canoe).

Today, New Zealand has not just three islands, but is an archipelago comprising over 700 offshore islands, most of which are small and lie within 50 kilometres of the coast. The islands are actually the visible surface of an extensive submarine plateau, Zealandia, a continent that is 93 per cent submerged. While most people are aware of the North, South and Stewart Island (Rakiura), there are other inhabited islands – Waiheke Island in Auckland's Hauraki Gulf, Great Barrier Island, east of the Hauraki Gulf, and the Chatham Islands, which are 800 kilometres east of the South Island. The Realm of New Zealand also includes the Cook Islands and Niue, which are self-governing but in free association, Tokelau, and the Ross Dependency (New Zealand's territorial claim in Antarctica).

Noted for its geographic isolation, New Zealand is about 2000 kilometres away from both Australia and Polynesia and, at just under 270,000 square kilometres, is a little smaller than Italy and Japan and a little bigger than the United Kingdom. It is more than 1600 kilometres long with approximately 15,000 kilometres of coastline, one of the longest in the world.

New Zealand's climate is mild and temperate, mainly maritime, although there are many regional variations and the weather has a distinct unpredictability. Northern regions are at an equivalent latitude to the south of Spain, and Auckland and the northernmost parts enjoy a warm, subtropical climate. The South Island's West Coast can catch some furious storms and is extremely wet, while conversely the east coast experiences long, dry summers and many droughts. In the far south of the South Island, the latitude is reflected with cold temperatures and the long summer days and winter nights of regions closer to the poles.

With a population of around four million, it is one of the least crowded countries in the world, and more than 85 per cent of the population live in urban areas. The capital city is Wellington, while Auckland is the largest and most populated. Other major urban centres include Christchurch, Hamilton, Napier–Hastings and Dunedin.

While the North and South islands are separated by only 20 kilometres of water, they have quite different landscapes. Millions of years of volcanic activity in the north have left a distinctive legacy of cones and lava flows. The Central North Island consists of a complex landscape of extinct, dormant and active volcanoes – Mts Ruapehu, Tongariro and Ngauruhoe dominate that part of the island, with extensive geothermal activity in the area, and Rotorua's mudpools and geysers are a huge tourist attraction.

West of here the Taranaki region is also dominated by the large volcanic cone of Mt Taranaki, which was last active around 250 years ago. The East Cape, in contrast, is a remote, mountainous domain with a spectacular coastline of bluffs and beaches. Further south, Hawke's Bay – with the two main towns of Napier and Hastings – is a different visage again, with broad plains, vineyards and large pastoral runs.

The lower North Island is divided by the forested Rimutaka and Tararua ranges, with the fertile plains of the Wairarapa on the east, and Manawatu, Horowhenua and greater Wellington on the west.

Stepping foot on the South Island, you are immediately aware of a very different landscape, as mountaineer Harry Scott discovered when he arrived in 1950. He wrote:

> I felt immediately and overwhelmingly that I had come to a quite different country …. Here then was a vast kind of land, whatever its size on the map, giving a sense of great distance where herds of grazing animals might roam, where grain plants might grow and a people wander. This had always been for me the meaning of continents.

The northern tip of the South Island is the Nelson–Marlborough region, housing three national parks, the stunning Marlborough Sounds, and Golden Bay's internationally recognised Farewell Spit – a feeding and breeding ground for migratory and endemic birds.

The South Island is divided along its length by the Southern Alps, which rise in parts over

Wellington

The nation's capital is a cosmopolitan city with Pacific, Asian and European communities and is the second largest urban area. It is the country's political and financial centre – home of the Parliament and accompanying government departments and major companies. It was actually built across a major fault line and is prone to small earthquakes. Wellington's reputation is as New Zealand's centre for music and the arts, and it enjoys a multitude of galleries, cafes and restaurants.

Christchurch

With a population of approximately 500,000 people, this city is the major urban area of the South Island. It is Canterbury's major commercial centre and houses an international airport, university and other cultural institutions. It has a definite English feel to it with the rivers Avon and Heathcote, its gothic and Victorian architecture and the Anglican cathedral.

Dunedin

Once New Zealand's richest city due to the gold rush in the 1860s, Dunedin is today a mellow city that's nurturing a strong arts side – it has thriving music, arts and fashion scenes due to the high proportion of students within its population. It is sometimes referred to as the Edinburgh of the South, due to the many Scots who settled there and the fact that the name is derived from the Gaelic for Edinburgh.

Stewart Island

Stewart Island is mainly low rugged hills and, unlike the two main islands, it remains almost entirely covered in native vegetation. It is bigger than many people think – 64 kilometres long and 40 kilometres at its widest point, with 700 kilometres of coastline. A large expanse of water, Paterson Inlet, almost cuts the island in half, and near its entrance is the island's only settlement, Oban at Halfmoon Bay, with around 380 permanent residents.

The eastern lowlands of the island are forested, with kamahi, rimu and miro trees housing impressive numbers of kaka, parakeets, tui and bellbirds. Kiwis are found all round the island. Mason Bay, on the west coast, is a 12-mile crescent of sandy beach, with huge sand-hills and tussock and scrub.

3000 metres, and include New Zealand's highest peak, Aoraki/Mt Cook at 3754 metres. To the west of the Alps is the West Coast, spanning 600 kilometres from Karamea down to the Cascade River, an area of wild beauty and uncompromising environments. It remains the least modified area of developed New Zealand, and much of it is protected not only for its scenic value, but for its considerable ecological significance.

In sharp contrast, to the east are the Canterbury plains, smoothed by over a million years of wind, water and ice age glaciers, and creating the largest expanse of flat land in New Zealand. In South Canterbury there is the country's highest cluster of mountains in Aoraki/Mount Cook National Park, while Banks Peninsula juts out into the Pacific Ocean, formed when two volcanoes stopped erupting about five million years ago.

The deep south of the South Island is celebrated for its stunning mountain and lake scenery. In the west it houses the mountains of Fiordland and Mount Aspiring national parks, while to the north it has the plateaux and valleys of Central Otago. The great southern lakes of Te Anau, Manapouri, Wanaka, Hawea and Wakatipu, along with the national parks, are now part of a World Heritage Area.

Its past

New Zealand has a shorter human history than any other country. Tangata whenua – the first people of the land – were the Polynesians, who arrived in New Zealand between AD800 and 1300. These earliest settlers are usually referred to as moa hunters, as the moa, a huge flightless bird, offered them a food supply unequalled in size in Polynesia.

These first people seem to have been nomadic hunter-gatherers who had neither weapons of war nor fortified living places. They lived off the then plentiful fish, birds and shellfish and lived reasonably well. They brought with them kumara (sweet potato) and yams.

They also brought a mythology of a land that was living and peopled with gods, and developed a culture that wove close connections between human beings and the mysterious and powerful forces of nature and the spirit realm.

Society was organised around groups that traced their descent from common ancestors, and reciting whakapapa (genealogies) was an important way to pass down that knowledge. Land was communally owned, and to take or use the earth's resources would often necessitate the use of special rituals or prayers.

These people did not identify themselves by a collective name and it was only with the arrival of the Europeans that they began to distinguish themselves with the name Māori, meaning 'ordinary'. The name they gave to these new settlers, the Europeans, was Pakeha, or 'foreigner', and the word is still used today to describe non-Māori New Zealanders.

Dutch explorer Abel Tasman was the first European to arrive – he and his crew came looking for the riches of a great southern continent in 1642. But, despite charting part of the west coast of the South Island, Tasman left without setting foot on the islands following a skirmish with the Māori in what is now Golden Bay. Aotearoa became a jagged and incomplete line on European maps and gained its name of Nieeuw Zeeland, but it was to be over a century before another European would visit.

In 1769 the British navigator James Cook circumnavigated and mapped New Zealand over three voyages, completing a remarkably accurate and detailed chart of the coastline. He returned to Britain with news of this bountiful land, paving the way for the country's subsequent colonisation.

First to arrive were the traders and hunters, keen to exploit the country's natural riches of timber, flax, whales and seals. By the early 19th century some began to settle, and some to farm. Next to arrive were the missionaries, concerned about the increasing lawlessness and immorality of the early trading communities. From these missionaries Māori learned not just about Christianity but also about European farming techniques and trades, and how to read and write.

While Christianity would become important for Māori, they were slow to convert. Trading their flax and potatoes for muskets had a greater impact in the 1820s and 1830s than religion, and escalated the killings in tribal conflicts. But diseases introduced by Europeans caused more fatalities than firearms, and the Māori population dwindled rapidly.

While the North Island was immersed in the Land Wars of the 1860s and 1870s, when colonial troops and Māori fought over the sale of land to settlers, the South Island was generally peaceful. Sheep and gold were to be its financial backbone, with a gold rush in the 1860s.

Following an economic depression with unemployment and emigration to Australia, New Zealand's economy was given the boost it needed with successful shipment of frozen meat in 1882. In effect New Zealand then became a British farm, exporting meat and chilled butter and cheese and, with an economy based on agriculture, the landscape was transformed from forest to farmland. Refrigerated shipping was to remain the basis of New Zealand's economy until the 1970s.

Treaty of Waitangi

In 1840 Britain claimed sovereignty of New Zealand as a colony, and William Hobson, the first governor of New Zealand, was sent from Britain to negotiate a treaty with Māori. The result was the Treaty of Waitangi, a document remarkable in that, unlike the colonisation in other parts of the world, it did not attempt to extinguish or enslave the indigenous people. Instead, it attempted to gain legal control of New Zealand with the consent of Māori chiefs, and guaranteed that individual Māori iwi (tribes) should have undisturbed possession of their lands, forests, fisheries and other taonga (treasures).

The Treaty was taken all round the country, as far south as Foveaux Strait, for signing by local chiefs, and eventually more than 500 signed.

However, the drafting and translation were done quickly and inexpertly, and, while the Treaty is seen as New Zealand's foundation as a nation, it is widely regarded by Māori as having not been honoured. Accordingly, the Waitangi Tribunal was set up in 1975 to address these grievances, and the Crown is now part-way through negotiating substantial settlements with many different tribes.

Political time-line

1852 – New Zealand Constitution Act was passed, setting up a central government with an elected House of Representatives and six provincial governments.

1890 – New Zealand's first 'modern' political party, the Liberals, came into power and over the next ten years or so oversaw policies of buying Māori land in the North Island and offering advances to settlers.

1893 – New Zealand became the first country in the world to give women the vote, following a nationwide campaign led by Kate Sheppard.

1907 – New Zealand is styled a dominion rather than a colony.

1912 – William Massey led the Reform Party to power, promising state leaseholders they could freehold their land.

1916 – Labour Party is formed.

1920s – Great Depression throughout the world hits New Zealand hard with farmers facing difficulties and urban unemployment figures high.

1935 – Labour Party swept to power under Michael Joseph Savage.

1936 – State housing programme begins, effectively the start of the welfare state.

1949 – Labour lost power to the conservative National Party, which, apart from two single-term Labour governments in 1957–60 and 1972–75, ruled until 1984.

1983 – The term 'dominion' is replaced by 'realm'.

1984 – Labour elected to power.

1990 – National Party in power.

The First World War was to have an effect on New Zealand – it rallied behind Britain, sending troops overseas, and to their death. In particular the 1915 landing at Gallipoli in Turkey was a coming of age for the country, and established the tradition of ANZAC (Australian and New Zealand Army Corps). New Zealand troops also fought and died on the Western Front. Again, in the Second World War New Zealand troops fought in support of Britain.

During the Pacific War of 1941–45 the United States, not Britain, protected New Zealand against the Japanese. After the war, in 1951, New Zealand joined the United States and Australia in the ANZUS alliance.

Following World War II, several movements emerged to challenge the conservatism of mainstream New Zealand culture – the Māori protest movement was one. And in 1981 the country was polarised amid some of the most violent protests New Zealand has ever seen. The issue at heart was a tour by South African rugby team the Springboks, whom many felt shouldn't be allowed in because of the country's apartheid policy. Following the tour, New Zealand didn't have official sporting contact with South Africa until the early 1990s.

Today, while New Zealand still has very strong links with Britain, it is seen as a Pacific nation with an independent outlook, willing to take an unpopular political stance because of its views. In 1984, for example, it adopted a no-nuclear policy, which means no nuclear-armed or propelled ships were allowed to enter its ports. This effectively ended New Zealand's participation in the ANZUS alliance.

Its people: Immigrants

From the earliest Polynesian settlers of around 1000 years ago, to the recent influx of south-east Asians, people from all over the world have been settling in New Zealand – a country envied for its lack of crowds, stunning scenery, quality of life and egalitarian attitude.

But it wasn't always seen as such an appealing place to live – 50 years after Cook had charted the country, only 200 new settlers had made the long journey to what was seen by most Europeans as a strange and lonely land at the other side of the world. However, the New Zealand authorities began promoting the country as a great place to start a new life – an early marketing plan if you like – and offered free, or assisted, passages to people willing to settle.

For over 130 years, from 1840 to the 1970s, New Zealand had a clear aim to populate its islands with 'kith and kin' from the United Kingdom. The early schemes to attract settlers had a focus on bringing over agricultural workers and domestic servants, with significant numbers of people arriving over a fairly short period: the population of non- Māori jumped from just 2,000 in the early 1800s to 250,000 in 1870. The most significant period of immigration was between 1871 and 1885 when almost 290,000 people arrived (although 40 per cent did move on).

The Great Depression hit New Zealand in the 1880s and 1890s and, as economic conditions worsened, newcomers who were not Anglo-Saxon were not welcomed. In 1899 a law imposed an English-language restriction on all immigrants not of British or Irish parentage.

This clearly racist attitude towards immigration was to remain an unsavoury element of New Zealand's policies during the early 20th century, and when World War I broke out, suspicion towards outsiders intensified. Legislation was passed to try and establish 'white only' immigration – 98 per cent British was the decree.

This was the pattern for the years between the wars, but by 1935 the Department of Immigration had been shut down and New Zealand's doors were effectively closed. However, 1947 saw the arrival of yet another assistance scheme when there was a demand for skilled workers and, over the next 30 years, it would bring over 100,000 people to New Zealand. As ever, assistance went primarily to British citizens of 'European race and colour'.

To say that only whites were allowed to enter, however, would be misleading. Asians had been arriving, particularly from Thailand, Malaysia and Indonesia, since the 1950s and by 1972 there were also over 50,000 Pacific Islanders in the country. By 1971 the proportion of New Zealand's foreign-born population who were from countries outside the white British Commonwealth was 30 per cent – double that of 20 years before. As the colour of the population changed, so did attitudes.

New Zealand was forced to confront its racist past and immigration policies were changed – no longer would the focus be on race or colour, but based on individual skills and qualifications. In 1975 assisted immigration from Britain was formally ended.

Since the 1970s New Zealand's population has gone through some dramatic changes – significant influxes of Pacific Islanders have arrived, and the country has also accepted refugees from Asian countries such as Cambodia, Laos and Vietnam and, more recently, Myanmar (formerly Burma). Political crises in Africa and the Middle East have also added a distinctive culture to New Zealand's bigger cities – Iranians, Iraqis and Somalians, as well as Afghans, have arrived and settled.

During the 1990s there have been large numbers arriving from other parts of Asia – Koreans, Japanese and Chinese – some coming for education, or to transfer their skills to a country less crowded than their own.

The 2006 census revealed how these more recent migrations to New Zealand are impacting

1996 – New Zealand inaugurates a new electoral system, Mixed Member Proportional, which increases representation of smaller parties.

1999 – Labour outpolls National and forms a coalition, minority government with the left-wing Alliance party. Helen Clark is Prime Minister.

Since 1999 there have been two elections, with Labour each time forming alliances with parties including United Future, Progressive Coalition and New Zealand First.

Kiwi character

What is a typical New Zealander like? Like any nationality there are stereotypes and myths, but it would be fair to say that there are some definite national characteristics of New Zealand citizens – a sense of fair play, distaste for class distinction, and a concern for the underdog. The Kiwi character is also something of a rugged individualist, a resourceful, inventive type who, in a reference to the rural roots of many New Zealanders, is said to be able to make anything out of a bit of 'Number Eight fencing wire'. This do-it-yourself approach is an echo of the pioneering self-sufficiency required when commodities had to come from half the world away.

New Zealanders are also well known for their genuine friendliness, interest in visitors and their laid-back attitude to life. Their geographic isolation means they are interested in what is happening elsewhere in the world, and they are avid travellers. The Overseas Experience (commonly referred to as the OE) is a very common 'ritual' for young people, who mainly head to the United Kingdom to work and base themselves for travel around Europe and further afield. While the majority do come home to settle, there are thousands of expatriate Kiwis living all round the globe.

on the ethnic make-up: while Europeans remained the largest ethnic group, at 2.6 million people, Māori number over 565,000, and Asians at almost 355,000 – the fastest increase since 2001. Pacific Islanders numbered almost 266,000. These newest settlers have transformed the nation's cultures and values and no longer is New Zealand seen as a far-flung outpost of Britain, but as a modern and diverse Pacific island nation.

Its people: Māori

As the first settlers of New Zealand, the Māori have had to undergo and deal with huge changes in their lifestyle and environment over a relatively short period of time – watching as their ancestral homeland has been colonised and settled.

Pre-European Māori, as described earlier, lived communally and in tribes and sub-tribes, and had a very different approach to land than the Europeans – they owned it communally. The arrival of the new settlers introduced to the indigenous people a new economy which some readily accepted with many iwi becoming quite wealthy.

But the Māori people were badly affected by various factors – disease, land confiscation and social dislocation had drastically reduced their numbers from 100,000 in the early 19th century, to just 50,000 within 100 years.

This declining population and dwindling resources as their land was taken and sold to settlers meant the Māori had less of an influence on how the country was run. Important Māori leaders became prominent during this period, and in the late 1890s the Young Māori Party was formed. One leader, Sir Āpirana Ngata, was typical of those among the indigenous people who were determined to rejuvenate the Māori people, society and culture. The period between 1900 and 1950 is dominated by the work of Ngata and his group, which included entry into Parliament, the reform of land tenure arrangements, and health reforms.

Most Māori continued to live in remote rural communities until World War II, following which they moved to urban areas to find work. During the late 1960s there was a growing awareness of the impact of colonisation on Māori, and they began to make their protests heard. Movements such as Ngā Tamatoa (the young warriors) emerged in the 1970s and, along with mainly other urban groups, they led the moves to raise awareness of the loss of land and culture.

A land march in 1975, led by Dame Whina Cooper, saw thousands of Māori from all over the country walk the length of the North Island, from Te Hāpua to the nation's capital, Wellington.

A couple of years later, the Ngāti Whātua tribe, who had been evicted from Okahu Bay in Auckland in 1951, occupied Bastion Point.

In 1975 the Waitangi Tribunal was established to consider claims by Māori of injustices under the Treaty of Waitangi and recommend action to the government: in 1985 the tribunal's powers were widened to allow it to hear claims dating back to 1840. The Waitangi Tribunal's vision states: '…having reconciled ourselves with the past and possessing a full understanding of the Treaty of Waitangi, Māori and non-Māori New Zealanders will be equipped to create a future for two peoples as one nation.' Claims are still being heard today.

Over the past 30 years there has been a remarkable renaissance of Māori culture, with the establishment of a Māori language system (see pull out box on Te Reo), the rearrangement of Māori-owned assets and industry initiatives such as aquaculture and farming in Māori ownership. Politically they have much more representation than they have ever had.

That said, they have numerous challenges – certain diseases such as diabetes and heart disease are more prevalent among Māori. Unemployment rates have been consistently higher than for Pakeha, and housing in certain parts of the country is poor.

Biodiversity

'Whatu ngarongaro he tangata, toitu he whenua' is a traditional Māori proverb, which translates to: 'man perishes, but the land remains'. While this is true from a human perspective, the solidity of the rock beneath our feet in New Zealand is less sure when looked at from a geological basis.

New Zealand is, in geological terms, a young country and was born out of a major collision between two of the earth's plates some 500 million years ago. At the time the ancient land masses of Australia, Antarctica, Africa and South America were all joined as one single giant southern continent now called Gondwana. As it began to break up, the land we now call New Zealand became a separate archipelago, moving further and further away from its neighbours. It broke away from its last Gondwana connection, Australia, some 70–80 million years ago.

For most of its above-sea history, 80 per cent of New Zealand has been covered with diverse and evergreen forests. The two main types are:

- Podocarps, an ancient family of trees, including rimu, kahikatea, matai and totara that have changed little in the last 190 million years. In the north of the country the podocarp forests were dominated by the huge kauri trees, among the largest in the world that could reach 1000 years old and more.

Te Reo (Māori language)

In 1987 the Māori Language Act came into force and did three things: declared the Māori language an official language of New Zealand; allowed Māori to be spoken in courts of law, commissions of inquiry and tribunals; and established Te Taura Whiri I te Reo Māori (Māori Language Commission). It promotes the use of Māori as a living language and as an ordinary means of communication.

Māori is the ancestral language of the original settlers in New Zealand and was one of the taonga (treasures) protected under the Treaty of Waitangi. In more tangible terms, the Māori language is seen as a powerful social force for the reconstruction of a damaged and deteriorated self-image among Māori youth, and a means of retaining dignity.

To help reverse the drastic decline in the numbers of people speaking Māori, one of the most visible and widely felt changes has been the establishment of kōhanga reo, or language nest, which immerse children in te reo Māori. The first one was set up in 1981, and within 15 years kōhanga reo was the single largest provider for children enrolled in early childhood education.

Today, many formerly European place names are known by their Māori name – eg Mt Egmont is now Mt Taranaki.

Some Māori words

Haere mai! – welcome, enter
Iwi – people, nation, tribe
Whanau – extended or non-nuclear family
Kai – food
Kia ora – hello, good day, (thank you)
Marae – the area for formal discourse in front of a meeting house, or applied to a whole marae complex

- Southern beeches, a less diverse family of which New Zealand has four species.

The dominant inhabitants of the forests were birds and, with a lack of predator mammals, non-fliers such as the kiwi, kakapo and the moa could survive. The moa were the prey species of a giant eagle, or Haast's eagle, a bird so large it would have dwarfed a condor. Both the moa and the eagle became extinct after the arrival of humans in New Zealand.

The emblematic kiwi, a shy nocturnal flightless bird that is endemic to New Zealand, fills the role of a small forager of the leaf-litter. It is not known when or how the kiwi came to the country, but some theories point to it being an ancient import from Australia.

Until 2006 it was thought that no mammals, other than bats and marine mammals, had reached New Zealand before humans did. However, the discovery of bones of an extinct mammal in Otago, dated to between 16 and 19 million years old, has changed the view of the country's evolutionary history, as it suggests mammals had been part of New Zealand's fauna since the break-up of Gondwana. It is not known why, or when, land mammals became extinct.

New Zealand's long isolation means that three quarters of its remaining indigenous flowering plant species are unique to this country. It has a high number of endemic species: all reptiles, bats and native amphibians, as well as 90 per cent of freshwater fish are only found here. It also has two sub-species of endemic cetaceans, the Hector's dolphin and its close relative Maui's dolphin.

The tuatara is a unique component of New Zealand's biodiversity – a prehistoric, direct descendant of the dinosaur, it is a reptile that can reach up to a metre long, complete with vestigial third eye.

Since the arrival of humans, New Zealand's natural world has suffered more decimation than that wrought by ice, volcanic eruption or earthquake. The heavy hand of the settlers – making fires, clearing the land for agriculture, and felling trees for timber – caused huge, irreversible damage. The great kauri forests of long ago were practically wiped out; some 1.2 million hectares had been reduced to just 200,000 by 1900. The tree is now protected and cannot be milled.

The humans also brought, intentionally or otherwise, a raft of pest species, such as rats, stoats and possums, which not only detrimentally affect the native vegetation, but prey on the indigenous species. Over half of New Zealand's pre-settlement bird species are now considered extinct and what remains are among the most threatened in the world.

However, in the 20th century New Zealand has been aggressively protecting its natural environment and biological heritage and has undertaken some pioneering work to do so. The

Department of Conservation (Te Papa Atawhai), known commonly as DOC, was set up in 1987 from many previous conservation agencies. Its aim was to 'protect natural and historic heritage, and provide recreational opportunities on land entrusted to its care.' It is working hard throughout the country to manage and eradicate introduced pests, and to encourage the restoration of natural habitat where native species can hopefully flourish in the absence of predators.

National Parks

- Tongariro National Park, established in 1887, the country's first, which includes the three active volcanoes, Ruapehu, Ngauruhoe and Tongariro.
- Te Urewera National Park, established in 1954, is the largest remaining area of native forest in the North Island.
- Egmont National Park, established in 1900.
- Whanganui National Park, established in 1996.
- Kahurangi National Park, established in 1996, includes the Heaphy Track and is the second largest.
- Abel Tasman National Park, established in 1942, is New Zealand's smallest at 225 square kilometres.
- Nelson Lakes National Park, established in 1956.
- Paparoa National Park, established in 1987, it includes the celebrated Pancake Rocks at Punakaiki.
- Arthur's Pass National Park, established in 1929, straddles the main divide of the Southern Alps.
- Westland/Tai Poutini National Park, established in 1960, includes glaciers, scenic lakes and dense rainforest.
- Aoraki/Mount Cook National Park, established in 1953, contains New Zealand's highest mountain Aoraki/Mt Cook. Together the Westland/Tai Poutini and Aoraki/Mount Cook national parks have been declared a World Heritage Site.
- Mount Aspiring National Park, established in 1964.
- Fiordland National Park, established in 1952, is one of the largest in the world at 12,519 square kilometres, and is also a world heritage area.
- Rakiura National Park, established in 2002 on Stewart Island/Rakiura.

National Parks

Almost one third of New Zealand's land – more than 80,000 square kilometres – is in protected areas comprising national, forest, wildlife, marine and historic parks and reserves, which are administered by DOC.

Included in these protected areas is a network of 14 national parks, the first of which was established in 1887, and which together account for just under 25,000 square kilometres of land.

In 1980 the National Parks Act was passed to establish parks or reserves in areas where the scenery is of such distinctive quality, or the natural features or ecological systems are so important scientifically that their preservation is in the national interest. The act also provides for the public to have freedom of entry and access to the parks.

Culture

Contemporary New Zealand has a diverse culture with influences from European, Māori, Australian and American cultures, along with Asian and non-Māori Polynesian. Large celebrations of Indian Diwali and Chinese New Year are held in Auckland and Wellington, as is the world's largest Polynesian festival, Pasifika.

The profound change in New Zealand's ethnic make-up in the latter part of the 20th century has been reflected in the arts too, from the creation of home-grown television programmes, to the Polynesian influence on popular music, as well as a resurgence of Māori traditional and contemporary arts.

Like any other nation it has its icons and emblems: the images and objects that have been made symbols of national identity, such as the kiwi bird, the fern frond, pavlova dessert and Marmite spread. But these are only emblems – creative activities such as visual arts, music, literature and design are central to New Zealand's identity.

Historically, the Māori developed a tribal culture based on their Polynesian origins, adapted to their new home, and their knowledge and arts formed a unique interpretation of the world as they knew it.

With the arrival of the Europeans came new cultural values and a completely different idea about the place of art in society. The accepted educated view of the time was that New Zealand's culture was an antipodean (and inferior) version of Britain's.

Thankfully, in recent years, the arts in New Zealand have flourished, supported and financed by successive governments, and it now has a distinctive culture with its own identity and feel and can boast many artists of international stature. Novelist Keri Hulme, film director Peter Jackson and singer Dame Kiri te Kanawa are just a few who are household names throughout the world.

Once artists would have had to go overseas to make a living – and some still do – but the growth of public and private support for the arts in the last 60 years means many can stay in their homeland and be successful.

In 1991 the Ministry for Cultural Affairs was established, and it is spearheaded by Creative New Zealand (The Arts Council of New Zealand: Toi Aotearoa). Festivals showcasing everything from chamber music to 'wearable arts' have become regular events, the best known being the biennial New Zealand International Arts Festival, which began in 1984 in Wellington. A new national museum, Te Papa Tongarewa, opened in Wellington in 1998.

New Zealanders like art – a 2002 survey found that 36 per cent had bought an original work of art or craft in the previous 12 months, while almost half had visited a gallery or museum. Artists such as painters Colin McCahon and Bill Hammond, sculptors Neil Dawson and Jacqueline Fraser, photographers Anne Noble and Lawrence Aberhart, and glass artist Ann Robinson have a strong following.

Māori artists have increased in number and influence since the 1970s, when Ngā Puna Waihanga (the Association of Māori Arts and Writers) began. A landmark event was the Te Māori exhibition of 1984 which took traditional Māori art to the world and also opened the eyes of New Zealanders to what was being produced.

As part of the recent resurgence of Māori culture, the tradition-based arts of kapa haka (song and dance), carving and weaving are widely practised, and the architecture of the marae maintains strong links to traditional forms.

In the celluloid world of film-making, major international recognition for a New Zealand feature film came in 1993 when *The Piano*, directed by Jane Campion, won an Academy Award. And no one could deny that director Peter Jackson's Oscar-winning trilogy of films based on the *Lord of the Rings* books has had a huge influence in putting New Zealand on the world map. Another film which won international acclaim in the early part of this century was *Whale Rider*, which refers to the tale of Paikea, the Polynesian ancestor of the Ngāti Porou tribe, who arrived in New Zealand on the back of a whale.

As well as enjoying art, New Zealanders are avid readers. Locally funded public libraries are popular and well-used, and New Zealanders are reputed to buy more books per head of population than any other nation on earth. The country has produced a rich literature – writers from diverse cultural backgrounds include novelists Janet Frame, Keri Hulme, Maurice Gee and children's writer Margaret Mahy. Māori authors, writing in English, include poet Hone Tuwhare and novelists Witi Ihimaera and Patricia Grace. Local publishing houses, including university presses, operate in a small, competitive market.

New Zealand music is a vibrant expression of the culture of New Zealand and, while its origins lie in its colonial history, today it boasts a healthy and diverse collection of rock, hip hop, reggae, dub and electronica, alongside the more traditional folk music, brass and pipe bands.

Many of the country's more prominent mainstream bands have found their largest audiences in Australia, most notably Split Enz, founded in the early 1970s and including brothers

Tim and Neil Finn (who went on to form the hugely successful Crowded House). Recent bands and musicians achieving international acclaim include The Mutton Birds, Bic Runga, Shihad and The Datsuns.

Māori have also developed a popular music scene and incorporated reggae and other influences – most notable include Moana and the Moahunters and Fat Freddy's Drop.

However, it is in the world of sport that New Zealand has arguably made its name most prominently – the rugby All Blacks and cricketing Black Caps are prominent in their sports. Other popular sporting activities include netball, soccer, golf, ski-ing and sailing. Notable New Zealand sportspeople include horseman Mark Todd, rugby player Jonah Lomu and 2005 US Open golf tournament winner Michael Campbell. New Zealand is also considered a haven for extreme sports and adventure tourism – the world's first commercial bungee jumping operation was started in Auckland in 1986.

Economy

Today New Zealand's economy is a small but prosperous free market economy, greatly dependent on international trade, mainly with Australia, the United States of America and Japan.

For a developed country, New Zealand's economy is still very dependent on farming, although the old trinity of meat, dairy and wool has been supplemented by fruit, wine, timber and other products. Tourism is also a major industry, and the country has been successful in attracting several major film productions, most notably the *Lord of the Rings* trilogy.

Agriculture in New Zealand remains internationally competitive, despite its distance from the economic heartlands, because the farmers are technologically innovative and sensitive to market opportunities and change. The most important types of farming are: dairy; sheep; beef cattle; deer, goats and pigs; poultry; bees; crops; fruit and vegetables; and vineyards. Other products on the rise include cut flowers and olives.

Other primary industries include forestry, fisheries, energy (New Zealand is self-sufficient in all forms of energy except oil), coal, minerals (gold, silver and iron), and building.

While New Zealand's material output ranks fairly low compared to other countries, its climate, environment and relative security from war and terrorism mean that its inhabitants can achieve a very agreeable lifestyle. New Zealanders are generally well educated and healthy, and home ownership is an important aspiration for many New Zealanders.

Historically, New Zealand's natural resources were depleted, first by the Polynesian settlers, and then by the Europeans. In the 1850s and 60s, pastoralism developed, with large sheep runs mainly on the east coasts of both islands. In the long economic depression of the 1870s and 80s, many settlers left New Zealand, and the country's economic destiny seemed to lie in large-scale sheep farming and the export of wool, tallow and canned meat.

Refrigerated shipping opened up a new economy based on family farms, and forests were felled. Improved livestock were bred and freezing works and dairy factories efficiently turned out meat and dairy products for shipping to Britain. This made up 90 per cent of exports for the next 80 years or so.

Industrialisation in the early 20th century was forced by government intervention in order to generate jobs for the growing population, and a desire to reduce the dependence on exporting after the great depression of the 1930s. Auto assembly plants appeared, and hydroelectric dams began to provide electrical power. Following World War II, the economy recovered and there was a wool boom in the 1950s.

In late 1966, however, the export price of wool crashed with the increased competition offered by synthetic fibres, and meat exports came under pressure from white meats. The dominance of farm goods in New Zealand's economy came to an end.

Britain joined the European Economic Community in 1973 and, while New Zealand had already diversified its export trade, the loss of an assured market for farm products was a blow.

After two oil shocks in the 1970s, the National Government of Robert Muldoon prompted the so-called 'Think Big' industrial and energy projects in an attempt to keep New Zealand prosperous. However, the fall of oil prices in the early 1980s made these unsound, and inflation and unemployment mounted.

From the mid-1990s the New Zealand economy began to expand and at the beginning of the 21st century it continues to export most of its goods to Australia, United States, Japan, China and the UK.

New Zealanders continue to enjoy a reasonably high standard of living, but compared to many other Western countries the wages are low and the costs of living and buying property have increased dramatically in recent decades.

And, despite being known for their laid-back and relaxed nature, Kiwis are among the hardest working in the world – surveys have shown that about 40 per cent of employees work more than 45 hours a week, which is about the same as the UK and Japan. Some could argue that this strong work ethic is due to the historical Protestant ethic of the country, although it probably

Rogernomics

New Zealand was faced with some economic challenges in the early 1980s, so when Labour came into power in 1984, its Finance Minister Roger Douglas hastily put into place his Economic Policy Package – a raft of measures designed to reform the country's economic performance. This policy was, and still is, referred to as 'Rogernomics'.

Under the government's slogan of 'We will do the right thing', the reforms essentially dismantled the development of the previous 90 years and replaced it with a system based on American models. The financial market was deregulated, subsidies to many industries, notably agriculture, were removed or significantly reduced, and a tax on goods and services (GST) was introduced, initially at 10 per cent.

New Zealand was now part of the global economy and the focus of the economy shifted from the productive sector to finance. Approximately 76,000 jobs were lost in manufacturing between 1987 and 1992 and, during wage bargaining in 1986 and 1987 employers began to bargain harder, resulting in some below-inflation wage increases, in effect a pay cut in real wages.

Critics of Rogernomics say the reforms were put in place too quickly and without adequate thought, and that it failed to deliver the higher standard of living promised by its advocates.

simply reflects financial necessity. More recently, there have been moves to give New Zealand workers the right to negotiate greater work flexibility with their employers, and allow them to gain a better work–life balance.

They should perhaps take a leaf out of the book of Samuel Parnell, who campaigned for an eight-hour working day when he arrived in New Zealand from London in 1840. His movement caught on and new arrivals were met at the quaysides and told not to accept anything other than an eight-hour day. Although wages fell, it did remain the standard working day for most classes of labour.

Today, Labour Day, a statutory holiday since 1899, commemorates the introduction of the eight-hour day by Parnell and others in Wellington.

First published in 2007 by Craig Potton Publishing
98 Vickerman Street, PO Box 555, Nelson, New Zealand
www.craigpotton.co.nz

© Craig Potton Publishing

ISBN 978-1-877333-74-3

Additional text by Caroline Budge
Scanning by Image Centre, Auckland, New Zealand
Printed in China by Midas Printing International Ltd